Do You Know What It's Like?

MADAM LU

DEDICATION

To kids of all ages who may be feeling alone in life.
Please know that you really are not alone, that there are many people out
there who are experiencing similar feelings and emotions as you.

ACKNOWLEDGMENTS

I would like to express my great appreciation to all the many wonderful people in my life who have helped me, encouraged me, and saw me through this book. For my husband, Daniel, both my Mom, Barb and Mother-in-law, Ruthee, my children and all of my other family members and friends that have talked with me, read, offered comments, and assisted in the editing, proof reading and design.

Do You Know What It's Like?

Madam Lu

Do you know what
it's like to feel lonely?
Like no one is there
beside you...

...to lift you up
when you are feeling
blue...

...to help you go
another mile,

With a simple smile...

Do you know what it's
like to hide behind a
Smile?...

...when you are sad,
and have been for
awhile...

Do you know what it's like to have people say things about you that are not true?

Do you know what it's like
to be with someone you
thought liked you,
but in the end,
you come to find
they didn't?

Do you know what it's like
to have your heart broken
With words left unspoken...

...to hide the pain,
and wonder,

Will it happen again?

Most of all,
Do you know what goes on
inside of me?

then before you jump
to the judgement seat,
look a little deeper,
and maybe you will see...

the secrets of a
lonely girl...

...a lonely girl like me.

ABOUT THE AUTHOR

Hi, my name is Lacey, readers know me as Madam Lu. I was born and raised in a small town in southern Utah, USA Where I met my husband and we are currently residing in that same area. We have two children-One boy and one girl. They are very active and bring loads of joy to us every day!
I have always enjoyed writing poetry, and thinking of stories I want to write.
Most of my writing is based on emotions, thoughts, feelings or memories.
I also love being with family and friends, hiking, camping, 4wheeling, rappelling, rock climbing, swimming, music, art-mostly drawing and photography, Church, reading and sleeping....and of course Games of various kinds ranging from cards, to board games, video games and table top rpg (role playing games).
I am a Wife, a Mother, a Foster Mom, sister, daughter, cousin and friend. I am a writer, a poet, a photographer, artist and a believer. I am a "Mormon,"-a member of the Church of Jesus Christ of Latter Day Saints. I live it, I love it and I am grateful for it!
I write the things of my heart in hopes to help others.
It is my hope that people who are hurting or struggling in any way, will be able to see and know that they are not alone. There is help out there and all around, we just have to find the courage within ourselves to reach out and seek for that help.

NOTES

In the following empty pages, you may write the feelings, thoughts or emotions that you have. Anything that comes to your mind as you read this book.

_____

_____

_____

_____

_____

_____

_____

_____

_____

_____

_____

_____

_____

_____

_____

_____

_____

_____

Notes

Notes

Notes

Notes

Notes

www.ingramcontent.com/pod-product-compliance
Lightning Source LLC
Chambersburg PA
CBHW050920290526
45792CB00002B/823